Never Make the First Offer: Instead Ask How Much They Are Willing to Pay

Category: Business & Economics

Author: Bob Oros

Publisher: Bob Oros Publishing

ISBN: 978-1-387-19906-8

Copyright 2017

Description: If you must make the first offer, the more you ask for in the beginning, the better. You're not being greedy - you're being smart. Don't be shy when you state your original price - put on a show of confidence. Amateurs almost always hesitate when giving their first price and professionals very seldom do. Better yet, ask them how much they are willing to pay.

Key words: distributor sales training, food service sales, sales coaching, sales techniques, motivating sales people, job in sales, sales manager training, sales course, manufacturing sales training, wholesale sales training, online sales training, food sales jobs,

ISBN 978-1-387-19906-8

1. Why you should never make the first offer?

An experienced buyer will very seldom, if ever, accept your first price. An experienced seller knows this and always presents a price higher than they expect to get.

A buyer will feel like they are not doing their job if they don't get a sales person to move down a little on price. As a seller, if you don't give them a price reduction they will feel like you out-smarted them.

When someone asks you for a price on a single item that you know is price sensitive, try and get them to give you the price they are looking for.

For example: As you start looking up the price or waiting for your computer to boot up, you might respond with: "I'll be happy to give you a price on that, by the way, what price are you looking for?"

If you do get the buyer to tell you how much he or she is willing to pay, act slightly shocked as if their opening price is low!

When you are selling, always start at your highest price whenever possible. No matter what the customer may say (such as "This is a one-time only offer; take it or leave it!"), don't take it! If they really want to make the purchase, they'll move from that price.

Don't be shy when you state your original price - put on a show of confidence. Amateurs almost always hesitate when giving their first price and professionals very seldom do.

The more you ask for in the beginning, the better. You're not being greedy - you're being smart. Eventually you will meet an acceptable compromise, but usually not in the beginning.

When you ask for a higher price, you can always come down. If you begin by asking for a higher price and you know you will settle for the lower price, everyone comes out a winner. If you start low you may end up having to go ever lower.

Here's an example: I was in Ft Myers Florida taking a tour of Thomas Edison's winter home and workshop. The tour guide told a story I will never forget.

Thomas Edison had invented the "Ticker Tape" machine and was in the buyer's office in New York to sell it for use in the New York Stock Exchange. The buyer asked Edison how much he wanted for it. Edison said, "How much will you give me?" The buyer said "$25,000". Edison said, "I'll take it!"

Later they were having dinner and the buyer said to Edison, "you were mighty quick to jump on that $25,000, I would have paid all the way up to $50,000." Edison said, "I would have taken $5,000."

That was a great story – but I couldn't help but wonder. Edison must have been doing cartwheels in his mind thinking that he was getting FIVE TIMES MORE THAN WHAT HE WAS GOING TO ASK!   However, what if Edison would have said, "$25,000 – is that the best you can do?" The buyer might have gone up to $40,000.

Now Edison would really have a hard time concealing his excitement! Once again, what if Edison would have said "are you sure that is the best you can do – this is the only one like it in the world – it will do this and this and this?" The buyer might have gone up to $50,000."

Here is another real live example. I was at a convention sitting next to me was a gentlemen who had recently sold his company.   He told me how he started in his garage and built the business in to huge success.   When he went to negotiate the sale the buyers offered him thirty million dollars - he immediately took it. One year later they sold the company for SIXTY MILLION DOLLARS.

He said if he had only hesitated and not accepted their first offer he might have added TEN MORE MILLION to the selling price!

Of course, there may be times when you know what the competition has priced a certain item and to get the business you might go in with a lower price right up front. Other times you may be dealing with a regular customer and they might consider it a pain in the neck to have to negotiate a price week after week.

Remember the bottom line of your first offer is to view it as another tool in your strategy inventory. There are times when it would be unwise to give your lowest price first with nowhere to go - and there are other times when it would be unwise to give your highest price first as you might scare off a potential new customer.

However, if they make the first offer, you usually know which way to go on your counter offer.

Comments:

Before the first offer, be sure you have done your homework. Know the lowest price you can offer. To start at your lowest price leaves no room for negotiation, which is

8

probably, is not the smartest move. Sometimes that's ok, some customers just want your price; they don't have time or maybe the desire to play the back and forth negotiating game. Unfortunately many customers do not accept the first offer. Customers love to feel that they have got a deal! Start higher, negotiate- You win, the customer wins too.

Brooke Knight

It is true that these strategies are practiced worldwide. When I lived in Saudi Arabia, if you did not bargain with the shop keeper, they had no respect for you and would not come down from their highest price. If you did bargain with them, you earned their respect and their friendship, and eventually the lowest price.

Kimberly Burgess

Ahhhh in Poker (I mean sales) the adage has never been truer: The one who blinks first loses. This phenomenon is not limited to one vertical (sales) – it is true globally from the school yards, and sales offices all the way to World Peace Negotiations!

First Offer: there is NO way to avoid it; one of you HAS to go first.

Here are some strategies to help you through the process.

Strategies:

1) The Preemptive Strike – You go first and ask what price range they are looking in.

2) The Volley- You are asked first about price- use Bob's technique – lob the question back and inquire what range they are looking at.

3) The Double Volley- This can be a little tricky- They asked first, you lobbed it back and then they lobbed it back to you. If you don't answer this could go on a while and the end product will probably not be very productive. The best answer will be a range- State your High Number and you MID number. Don't let them have your bottom line.

4) The Slide: Here you go 1st and list a range (once again High to Medium) and ask where in that range they fall.

Let the negotiations begin.

NOTE: No strategy will work if you have not PREPARED before hand. You need to calculate what the highest (FAIR) profit margin number would be, what your mid point is and what is the lowest you can go and STILL be profitable. It is very important to know when the price/agreement is NO

LONGER BENEFICIAL to you and your company. You must be prepared to walk away when you reach this point.

Know when to hold them and know when to fold them,

Teresa Cloninger

I was working with a new salesperson. We went into an account where we knew it was going to be price sensitive. We gave them good prices on almost every item except for their number one item, chicken wings.

I knew from research before seeing this customer that he was getting a great price on this product. We were in the ball park but not where he is now. I knew he was proud of his price he was receiving. The new sales person wanted to go rock bottom on wings but I had another strategy.

I told him our pricing was fair and he would be happy with our proposal. BUT I said, ignore the wing price because I wanted to get more detailed information. After a few questions, he disclosed how much higher we were.

I then told him if we were good on the other pricing, I will need his help with our buyers to get the wing price. I made him feel proud of his wing price.

Our goal is to be competitive on all other items, and keep the same wing price that he is paying now. We could go lower but why?

Roland Degregorio

2. Why should you play dumb like a fox?

In buying or selling it is not always smart to be too decisive or knowledgeable. This is one of the classic strategies - it is well used by seasoned sales people.

Sometimes saying you don't know the answer or asking the customer what they think is far better than trying to wing it. Nobody has all the answers no matter how long they have been selling.

If the customer says "your price is high" simply say "I wonder why? Do you think the competitor is adding something in or taking something out that is making the price difference?" Ask to see the lable or the invoice so you can go back to your company and find the answers.

In other words - playing dumb can be smart.

This strategy is used to draw them out with the aim of extracting more information from them. You are up against a smooth customer when this is used against you.

You will get better answers if you are slow to understand. The trouble is that most of us want to look good. We find it hard to say, "I don't know" or "tell me that again."

An excellent example of asking for help: While I was sitting in a sales managers office getting ready to go to lunch with him, his secretary announced that his 11:45 life insurance appointment was here. I volunteered to leave, but he said it would only take a few minutes and to stay put.

The young insurance man entered the office, handed the sales manager an application and said, "You don't want to buy any life insurance, do you?" That is considered the poorest choice of words a sales person could ever use.

The sales manager couldn't believe what he was hearing. He sat the insurance man down and for 15 minutes lectured him on how to sell. He told him how to use features and benefits, family protection, cash build up and education funds.

The sales manager said he was going to buy $250,000 additional coverage and began showing the young insurance man how to fill out the application. The sales manager handed the insurance salesman the completed application along with a deposit check and said, "Son, I hope you have learned never to use that opening question again?"

As the insurance man was leaving, his signed application and deposit check in hand, he turned to the sales manager and said, "Oh, I never use that line, unless I'm calling on a sales manager."

Customer surveys are basically useless because people only tell you what you want to hear. Here is a magic question that will reveal the true feelings of your customer: How can I make it better?

Q: How has our service been?

A: It has been fine.

Q: How can we make it better?

By using this additional question you are able to extract the real information you need. With this information you may be able to make changes or improvements before it's too late and you lose the customer to a more creative competitor.

Comments:

This is a proven effective strategy! This is extremely important to use on the customer who thrives on having their ego stroked as well. Saying things like, 'I'm not sure, what do you think?' make customers feel that you want to know what they think, their ideas, and suggestions. Playing dumb must be used with caution, as you never want to appear incompetent, no matter what type of customer you're dealing with. You must have some knowledge of your product, if you appear not to know what's going on do you really think you would be someone to trust to handle business with. Probably not…… Knowing when to use it is key.

Brooke Knight

The playing dumb strategy is a strategy that is taught to women growing up. Play dumb to men so that their ego is boosted and they will feel more important and they will feel that you need them. It usually works when I use it. I agree with Teresa (below) on this one, playing dumb could make you look incompetent to a client so you must use that strategy with caution. The last thing you want is to have the client think you are not smart enough to have his business.

Kimberly Burgess

PLAY DUMB -This one should come with a warning label "USE WITH CAUTION- IF NOT USED PROPERLY SERIOUSE HARM CAN OCCURE". You know like the labels on coffee from restaurants now- "Contents hot- may cause burning if spilled".

I completely agree on the asking open ended questions part- the more you ask the better informed you are. The

16

better informed you are the more sales you make! My philosophy is I am not selling you something; I am solving your problems. Sometimes, in order to learn what the customer's needs are (problems they are having), it's necessary to ask a few questions. The right questions can help your customer to open up to you, and give you some insight into how you can assist them. Some great questions to ask are:

1) What is the biggest obstacle you are facing right now?

2) If you could wave a magic wand, what would you fix?

3) Tell me about your past experiences using a similar service?

4) What do you hope will happen in the next 6, 12 or 24 months?

5) How will your business be changed by this?"

Teresa Cloninger

3. Are you implying too much flexibility?

For example, if someone asks for a price on 10 cases of a product you are selling, you would not want to say; "somewhere around $149" if the price was, in fact, $149. If you were presenting a price on a service you were selling and the price was $24.90 per hour you shouldn't say "somewhere around $25." By using the term "somewhere around" you have opened the door for the buyer to assume the price is flexible.

State the price firmly like you mean it. Many people don't state the price firmly and unknowingly open up the door for the buyer to start working on their price. Sometime the person presenting the price will do so giving a range rather that a firm price.

For example: "The price is between thirty five and forty dollars per case." This response signals a lack of confidence in the price quoted and encourages the customer to start working down the price, not from forty dollars, but from thirty five dollars.

Practice delivering your price with a tone of confidence. Deliver it with the same conviction that you would use to give someone your phone number.

"What are the last four digits of your phone number?"

5197 - Not "between 5196 and 5200".

What month were you born?

October - Not "somewhere between September and November".

If you signal with words such as "about" or "roughly,"' the buyer will take this to mean that you can go lower. If you do imply flexibility follow the other rule of selling - ask for more than you expect to get, because you may need the room.

Flexibility is a tool you can use - sometimes you might want to imply a certain degree of flexibility.

For example. Lets say a customer is looking for 100 cases of your product. You know that the customer has shopped around for a couple of other quotes. Giving your price too firmly may cause you to lose the business. However, giving your highest price and slightly implying that you are willing to work with the customer will open the door to a possible sale that would otherwise be lost.

But remember - flexibility is a tool - a strategy to use when the situation calls for it.

Comments:

When you quote someone a range, or a rough estimate just know they intend to start to work their way down from your bottom price. Not only that, they feel you have opened the door for "offers". That implies you have complete control over the price, this throws the higher authority strategy out the window. This is used on client by client basis too. If you know what the competitor has quoted room for negotiation may be necessary in gaining the business.

Brooke Knight

I don't believe that flexibility is weakness. When you're shaking about the price and you have little to no confidence in you or your product, then that is weakness. I do think that it's important to be firm in the price and know that the price you're giving them may be a little high but the service that YOU offer is more than well worth it. If you do decide to open it and sound flexible, be firm with it. Display the confidence that if you are willing to go down, it's because you want to help that customer and you're willing to work with them not because they control the situation.

Matthew Thacker

This articles points out something that I am instilling in people that are training. People are most sold by your conviction rather than your persuasion. People have to buy YOU before they buy from you. I think with practice and role play you can cumulate the confidence you need to quote rates with authority. It's the ease that comes from practicing or real life applicable experience.

Kristan Wilson

Look them in the eye as you give them the price. It is your product, be proud of it. Think of it as "spiking" the ball after a touchdown. You know this is the best product for your customer at a fair price. Be proud of it.

Do you think people who buy a Lexus are not looked in the eye when given a price? They know they are buying the best, a product with a track record. If they wanted cheep they would have gone to the "cheapo depo" and bought a older car, at a cheaper price with less or unknown dependability.
Trip English

You say flexible, translation weakness. Again, my hand goes in the air. I do have a problem with this, because one

22

senior salesperson says give the best price the first time, and another says start high and come down. And which is best, it depends on the client. Sometimes high price scares away potential business, but on the other hand if you give the best price first, there is no room for negotiation…again reading your client and getting as much information from them before providing any numbers is the only way to go.

Kathie Luttrell

There is no flexibility in menu prices at a restaurant so there should be no flexibility in proposing the cost.

A roast beef sandwich is not "about 7.99".

Roland Degregorio

4. When is the best time to make add on sales?

Beware of the person who agrees to your price too quickly, they may plan on asking for more.

If the buyer agrees to your price too quickly there is usually a request that will be close behind.

"That price sounds pretty good, I will take 100 cases."

"By the way can I have special terms on that?"

Another customer might agree to the price right away and ask for same day or next day delivery. From a buyers perspective this is called the "add on."

Agree to the initial price and then as soon as the sales person starts ringing up their commission, drop the "add on" question. This is an also an excellent strategy for you to use as a sales person.

Once you have what you want in hand, there is a natural tendency to leave as fast as you can. Perhaps there is an unconscious fear that the customer will change their mind or cancel the order - just the opposite is true.

Once a person makes a decision, their mind works to reinforce the decision. By getting a small commitment first the buyer will start to justify the decision and it becomes easier, not harder, to add on additional items.

Why? Think about your own decision making process. Once you make a decision your mind does a search, similar to a computer doing a search for additional information. Your mind is looking for ways to justify the decision you just made.

For example. Lets say you have made the decision to buy a new house. The mortgage payment will be much higher - but you justify it by saying that the new house will have three bedrooms for the kids, a two car garage so you can park both cars inside, a better school district, a dining room so we can have the family over for holiday meals, etc.

Then you get the news that the mortgage didn't go through.

You now justify the fact that you will really be better off without the higher mortgage, the kids are fine sharing a bedroom, the two car garage isn't really necessary, the school district is not that bad and I didn't really want to have the in-laws over for holiday meals anyway.

There is always supporting information for whatever decision you make. Notice the next time you have to convince your husband, wife or family member that you made the right decision about an important family issue. Your mind will make a mental checklist of the pro's and con's. If you are "pro" watch how your mind will weigh the list in your favor - especially if you have already made a decision and a financial commitment.

Your customer's mind works the same way. This tactic is being used on you every time you buy a car. First the car sales person will get you to agree on color, then options, then an extended warranty, and before you know it you bought the car - one small piece at a time.

The last-minute add on involves throwing in an extra request (usually not so huge as to break the sale but big enough to hurt) at the final moment, just when you, the sales person, has put down your defenses and assumes you have a deal.

The add-on seems to go against a person's nature. "I got what I wanted, I better leave before he or she changes their mind."

To successfully use this tactic, stick around a while. If you are selling multiple items, sell the first one. Wait a few minutes, sell the second one. Wait a few more minutes, sell the third one, and so on. Give the buyers mind a chance to justify their decision.

Remember, they are thinking, "I bought the first one - I might as well buy the second one. I bought the second one - I might as well buy the third one."

That is how little orders turn into big orders. It is like going into the grocery store and buying a chicken.

I bought the chicken - I better buy the potatoes - the salad - the rolls - the desert - and before you know it your shopping cart is full.

Comments:

I was taught to get the order signed and leave as quickly as possible. Some sales people will want to hang around and socialize for a while but this can give "buyer's remorse" time to kick in. If it happens when you are sitting in front of the customer it is very easy for him to retract or reduce his order. If you are not there he may feel that it is too late and start justifying his wise decision. However, I may have been leaving business business on the table by not adding something on immediately after he decided to buy.

Crocker Smith

I make my "add ons" during stages of my presentation. for example, "You will receive this service for $X dollars, Plus "add on, add on" at no additional cost." As we discuss more ideas and options I customize the "add ons" I fell would benefit that particular customer. The customer feels you are throwing something extra in!

Being on the other side of add on sales- Say you are about to close the deal when the customer throws in the extra request that cuts your commission half!! You must be able to justify with other benefits they are receiving as "no cost add ons" already. As sales people we are in it to make money, we just have to determine what we can take for the sale.

Brooke Knight

"It's a good strategy to have - but not advisable to do it all the time on the same customer or they will start to think that you are milking them. Be sure to only sell the customers what they want and/or need to grow their business. Sure, rolls are nice to have with a chicken dinner, but is it really necessary or critical to have? Over negotiating, or over selling your customer may also result in them looking for a new sales rep. This is once again a very delicate balancing act."

JoAnne Welch"

5. Ask for something in return for a price reduction?

Do not keep lowering your price without asking for something in return or you will make it too easy for the buyer to keep asking.

The trade off is a very basic yet important strategy when dealing with buyers. Every time you give in to one of the requests such as price reduction, marketing money, extra services, etc., the trade off strategy should go through your mind: "If I do that for the customer, what can I ask the customer to do for me?"

This is our attitude, not our actual statement. Negotiating as a seller is not the same as negotiating as a buyer. If you are selling and you get tough and walk away, at the end of the day you have not sold anything. Most of the negotiating strategies are designed for buyers and must be adjusted if used by a person trying to make a sale.

Many people complain that customers or buyers today have no loyalty. "Show a customer how to save money on a certain item and they will shop around to see if it can be purchased for a few cents cheaper from a competitor."

If customers are not loyal, perhaps it is because when you give everything you have, you do not ask for anything in return. Trading builds a relationship.

Giving and taking are part of selling; they are part of the process and not a sign of weakness! Here are a few points to keep in mind:

1. Do not assume the customer knows what you want. Make your request loud and clear! Do not be shy about asking for something in return when a customer asks you for a price discount. If it is done in a spirit of cooperation they will not take offence.

2. Whenever you give a price reduction, be sure to ask for something in return. You are not doing anybody favors by giving away something for nothing - the customer will not respect you and you hurt your self respect.

3. Make this an important principle in your selling. Never give up anything without getting something in return (even if what you get seems trivial). The customer offers to buy the floor model of the coffee machine at a reduced price. You, instead of lowering the price, offer a 90-day free service guarantee.

4. The customer requests a lower price on a larger than normal order. You offer some additional marketing support instead.

5. The customer complains that the price is too high. You offer to sell your higher quality product line at a slightly lower price. Explain to the customer that the higher quality is an investment in their customer satisfaction.

6. Whenever lowering the price, never go down in equal increments. If you have an extra five dollars built in, go down two dollars, and if you must go down a second time, reluctantly go down another dollar and twenty five cents, a third time go down a dollar and ten cents. Each time you go down on your price ask for an additional item or something else in return.

Comments:

Rather than lowering my price I have often said two things to a customer or a prospect. Well Mr. Prospect I know that this price is slightly higher than you are used to paying, but give me a moment to explain my Insurance policy to you (I sell food so this often takes them back for a moment). Anyone can come in with a low price but the real question is what are they offering. If the price is low and they can't provide quality for your customer or actually deliver the product because they don't use a consistent manufacturer, what in then end is a low price? It's you scrambling at the last minute. My fill rate and consistency of quality offer you an insurance policy you'll be happy to spend a few extra pennies on week after week. It's like walking in to your kitchen and knowing when you flip on the light switch your going to be able to start your day. If you simply want low price and no guarantees I can go back and discuss it with procurement. I rarely ever lower my price.

Michael S. Hutchison

"It's always a great idea to ask for something in return. My prospect, "if you give me the next shot at your business, I will reduce my price, but once you have benchmarked my service against your current service, we will then renegotiate my rates, does that sound fair?" Or you can use the scenario of a shortened liquidation period on the first order and then renegotiating those terms once you have your foot in the door. I once used this tactic to get business with UPS. We had 400 offices nation wide receiving our payroll checks and sending out payroll 2 times a week. I said, "if you give us the customer service business, we will switch our service from Fedex to UPS nationwide". It worked and my former company still uses UPS and they still staff UPSs Customer Service Departments."

Kristan Wilson

"In selling, the seller really does have the upper hand when it comes to negotiating the deal. The buyer will always try to low ball to see how much savings that they can get out of the deal. My sister currently has her house up for sale, and was offered a price that was $15,000 below the listed price.   I advised her to go back with the original price of the house ... but should the buyer want the house at the price that they had stated, it's going to come without the fridge, stove, washer, dryer ... etc. even down to the furnace!. All I can say is her real estate agent was shocked at her reply."

JoAnne Welch

"What do you suggest that we offer that is not already included in our sales pitch? We offer to handle payroll, worker's comp, counseling, customer service, drug screens, and criminal backgrounds – which is what every agency in this area also handles. What I am looking for is something that makes Ambassador stand up and above the rest – why should they choose my services over another company?"

Angela Brewer

"I agree, we come with the package. Not only are our clients buying our service but they get us. I tell them call me anytime if you have questions, problems, etc. I think them knowing we are available more than just regular 8-5 and are willing to go the extra mile, makes our office better than other temp services."

Sherry Tyner

"The first thing I think of in terms of trade-offs (with Ambassador) is our rate. If we lower our rate, we want to able to have more employees at that work site. If they only want one employee, we aren't going to be as willing to lower the rate. However, if they want 25 people, we can lower it substantially. Good advice, Bob."

Suzanne Davis

"You are right, often we forget and don't realize that we also have the power to negotiate. We get so locked into selling that we forget that we to can ask for something in return. Thanks for the reminder and it is my goal to try this with my next order."

Kathy Hart

"This is a great lesson I have seen this work. We have often gone down on price for larger quantities of orders. Such as 30 temps at a specified rate but should the number of employees decrease the rate will increase soon."

Crystal Brown

"This article reminds me of what the true art of selling is. Years ago people referred to buying a product from a company as "trading" with that company. Trading used to be the staple that built the relationship between the buyer and the seller. Today we are to eager to just buy or sell, and move on. There is very little trading that happens. If we begin to "trade" with our customers again, then we will build stronger, more loyal, clients."

Scott Green

"We had a customer that we got the contract even though our price was higher than the competitors. We provide employee staffing. We won the customers loyalty because we offered them more. We had a rate for the regular employees that we found for them, but if they had a person that they new and wanted to hire then we had a lower rate for them. Any time they needed more employees they new they could count on use to provide them with what they needed. We asked for them to call use for what ever their needs were and in return we gave them price adjustments."

Laura Rice

"I have used this recently in a sales call. She asked us for help in finding a particular type of person and asked if we were going to give her them. I said that it depended on what was in it for our company. Could we expect some orders from them? Also done this as a buyer in my husband's favorite store…Best Buy and it worked."

Linda Cassell

"For the most part, we do explain how we do not send just anyone for their positions. WE take the time to look for the correct person with the correct qualifications. I have done some trading when it came to direct hires, and it was in our benefit."

Pam High

"A lot of times agreeing to lower a bill rate will be agreed on if it means that we can get more temps out to this client which helps to balance out the agreement."

Marie Royal

"I believe I understand this concept well. The things I offer back or "trade off" with the customer are actually selling points to my service. For example, I offer ME, I offer insurance benefits when discussing payroll services, I offer delivery services when discussing temps, I offer personalized service and pick up and delivery of timesheets and checks all the time. There are many more options and trade off's we can offer. I learn a new one at least weekly. I also pay very close attention to my "higher authority" when she is with me and wheeling and dealing with the customer to learn what she offers."

Patsy Clements

"Should you ask for something in return for a price reduction? YES- Never give something for nothing. When a customer ask for a lower price ask for something in return no matter how small it might be. Or using product as a example give them a higher quality product at a reduced price and sale it as a quality to there customers."

Christal Cornacchia

"You should always ask for something in return if you are reducing your price. You are not doing anybody favors by giving away something for nothing – the customer will not respect you and you hurt your self respect. Giving and taking are part of the process and not a sign of weakness."

Stacy McDaris

6. How do you respond to a bait and switch?

Retail stores often advertise fabulous but fake bargains just to get you to come in so they can sell you something more expensive. This scheme is commonly referred to as "bait and switch."

It is simple enough: they advertise some item at a price low enough to lure you into the store. But here is the switch: the advertised item is not for sale. The salespeople may give you any number of reasons why you cannot or should not buy it.

"There are not any left. . ."

"Many customers who bought it are dissatisfied . . ."

"The product just is not any good . . ."

"You cannot get delivery for six months . . ."

The truth is that these salespeople never had any intention of selling the advertised special. They kill your desire to buy it and instead try to get you to buy the item they had in mind from the beginning.

"Bait and switch" is an unfair practice and is against the law. Although you cannot always spot bait ads in advance or know that the switch is going to follow, there are a few steps you can take to avoid the trap.

First, realize that a good salesperson may try to persuade you to buy a better quality item or a different brand with more features at a higher price.   There is nothing illegal or unethical about this. The important thing is that you are given a choice without undue pressure.

Keep in mind, though, that if a product or service is advertised at a price that seems too good to be true, this may be a bait ad. Then, if the merchant refuses to show you the advertised item, to take orders for it or deliver it within a reasonable time, disparages it, or demonstrates a defective sample of it, take this as a sign that you are probably being "switched."

For example: You go into a store to buy a computer you saw advertised. It was out of stock, but when a salesperson tells you a faster model is available for an additional $100, you purchased it because it was available immediately.

The deliberate use of stock outages of a featured, low-price bait brand in hope of persuading customers to switch to a more profitable substitute brand is a form of bait and switch.

If you want to see the bait and switch used, visit any car dealer. After you find the car you want you may be surprised to find your low offer immediately accepted. After getting you to commit yourself to a price the salesman will say something like, "Well this looks good." All I have to do is run this by my sales manager for approval and the car is yours:"

As you are sitting there congratulating yourself on getting such a good deal, the sales manager comes in to review the price with you. He says, "You know, Joe was a little out of line here. This price is almost $400 under our factory invoice cost." He produces an official-looking factory invoice. "You cannot possibly ask us to take a loss on the sale?"

Now you feel a little embarrassed. You are not quite sure how to respond. You thought you had a deal and Joe's bait and switch tactic just shot it down. If you stick to your guns and talk the sales manager into meeting your price, he will eventually cave in and tell you that since he is selling it under factory invoice he will have to get his manager's approval.

This game will continue as long as you can hold out against a battalion of managers.

Understand that it is a matter of perspective. While you may view this process as underhanded and deceptive, it is a time-honored negotiating tactic used everywhere in the world, from the Middle East bazaars to Mexican street markets.

Comments:

It is funny how this works to our advantage. I am in the produce business and customers regularly tell me that there are A,B,C grade produce available. I tell them that all my customers from the taco truck who picks up product every morning to the white tablecloth fine dining establishments get the same product. I tell them to come see the warehouse anytime. There is only one slot per product and it is all Grade A. There is no Bait and Switch. If that is what they have experienced give me thrity days. It will be a real eye-opener.

Dave Ferren

Bait and switch is a popular tactic used by chain appliance and electronics stores. Years ago in New Orleans I was looking for a new television. There was a locally owned chain appliance store that was always advertising items on sale. I remember several times seeing a 19 inch TV advertised at that store for $99 and in the small print it said brand would vary and 3 per store location. I went to the store just to check it out [I had already assumed it was probably a piece of junk but was curious]. When I asked a salesman about it he replied "You don't want that TV, it's a piece of junk. I do have a nice Sony on sale for $380 that you would be much happier with." He was honest at least about the low price TV being a piece of junk and I wouldn't have bought it anyway but the tactic turned me off so much I left the store. I ended up buying a TV at a different store later on.

Cary McAfee

My personal opinion is that although bait and switch is a long standing sales strategy. It is still under handed in my view. I would never use this tactic to sell a product. I feel that if this is used in your sales strategy then you may not have a product you believe in and shouldn't be selling it to begin with. Bait and switch can do nothing in the long run but damage your Company's and your reputation as a leader in your field

Brian Spraggins

Another problem with the bait and switch is that they trick you into thinking that they are looking out for your best interests, saving you from purchasing the lesser item. I heard on the radio the other day a local car dealer offering SUV's for 12,000 dollars, and then at the very end they said they only had two on the lot for that price. At least they admit to the bait and switch before you get there!

Morgan Frazier

I agree that most sales people do use the bait and switch. The most common place I have seen this is in the retail industry and it really depends on if you are buying for the price, or for the need. If you need the item you may opt to buy the higher priced item that is substituted. If you are buying a luxury item you may be a little more cautious. Shopping around before making any substantial purchase can usually help avoid a bait and switch.

Kathie Luttrell

I have always heard that car salespeople use this on a daily basis. This tactic was used on me at a dealership about eight years ago but in the legal way. The type of car I wanted was advertised at a price to entice any buyer to the dealership. Of course, this was the base model. Once all of the options were added, my monthly payment would have been $80 more per month. I contemplated for 2 days. The salesperson finally said, "Why don't you come and get your car". What are you going to do? I caved but I got the car I wanted.

Gregg Nixon

Bait and switch is not a tactic I would advise using in staffing, to be quite honest. The relationships we build with our clients are generally long lasting so it would do us little good to try and use a bait and switch tactic for a short term sale if we are trying to gain the long term business. Customers would not appreciate being duped.

In fact here in Beaufort it has done us good NOT to use that type of tactic. One of our competitors tried to lowball us by approaching our biggest customer and saying that they were less expensive. Our customer took the bait, and then when they received the invoice they discovered that while the markup was indeed lower than ours, there were several added fees that were not included in the markup (they were not informed of said fees) and it ended up costing more than us in the long run. Needless to say, they don't use that agency anymore and have been loyal to us for years. In fact they had enough trust to impart that story to us!!

Marquesa Ortega

I love it when a competitor uses a bait and switch on one of my customers. I inform them that they have fallen pray to a tactic used by some sales people and I apologize for my professions sleazy side. I then inform them that what the competitor did was give them an inferior product at a reduced cost. I show them that we also have cheaper products but that they have always purchased high quality products and I did not for see them wanting to lower their quality.

Patrick

I've worked for companies that thrived on the bait and switch. The jewelry industry does this on a daily basis and usually calls the bait a "loss leader". They will lose money on the advertised item(in hopes that you can switch)just to get you in the store. A skilled salesperson can make the switch;others sell many of the loss leaders. According to which side you're on,it can be a good tactic.

Rick Hughes

My daughter and I went to a clothing store recently. This article reminds me of what we encountered. This store had big red signed hanging all over the store that said "BUY ONE GET ONE FREE ON ALL CLERANCE". So my daughter and I said great, we could by get more for our money. So we picked out several items that we liked and went to check out. When the cashier started ringing up our items they were not ringing up "BUY ON GET ONE FREE". We asked the cashier what was going on and she said that the items we picked out were not included in the buy one get one free. We asked why and the excuse was that because they were considered blue jean material they did not count in the sale. So we argued that the sighs all over the store did not say that jeans were excluded. She then called someone else, and then the manager. We did not get the answers we were looking for so we told the manager that they could keep their merchandise and we would go to another store that did not have misleading sales signs everywhere. This was defiantly a "BAIT AND SWITCH".

Laura Rice

7. Why should you never split the difference?

As soon as someone suggests splitting the difference, the whole game changes.

The side that makes the offer has essentially revealed what they will settle for. You, a seller, should always let the buyer be the one to offer to split the difference first.

Suppose that after the initial negotiating, you a sales person, have a price of $50 per case on a one thousand case order and the customer wants to pay $45. The buyer says, "Let's split the difference." What they have just done is raised their offer to $47.50.

The negotiating range has changed. Before, the difference was $5. Now the difference is $2.50 per case.

What's your move? Acknowledge the offer with appropriate respect but make it clear that you cannot yet accept because the price is still too low. (Continue to maintain that the top of your limit is $50).

After waiting a few seconds, it becomes your turn to make a counter offer. But now the negotiating range is between $47.50 and $50.00. You say, "Let's meet half-way; I'll come down $1.25 and you come up $1.25."

The deal is struck at $48.75 per case. If you had been the one to offer to split the difference just the opposite might have happened. If you agree to split the difference you would have lowered your price to $47.50.

The buyer would have said to YOU: "Let's meet half-way; I'll come up $1.25 and you come down $1.25. The deal would have been struck at $46.25.

On a one thousand case order the difference would have been $2,500. (Which, of course, would have come out of your gross profit).

The first person who places a value on a product or service establishes its worth.

A perceived value must be established when the customr or buyer makes a low offer and gives you a low price. You should counter by presenting an equally high price. This is sometimes referred to as "bracketing."

Comments:

This all revolves around confidence in your selling abilities. I am, many times, tempted to take an offer of this type or to be the first to make the 'split the difference' offer to get the sale over with. This keeps the competitor from having another shot at the deal. However, as you stated, it can cost you profit. If you are always low bid you will eventually go out of business.

Crocker Smith

When you split the difference you are in most cases going to lose money. I can't afford that, can you? Place the value on your service, establishing its worth and benefit. We too are in business to make money; we can't lose profit to gain a customer every time. If we did we would not be in business....

Brooke Knight

About the author Bob Oros

Regardless of whether you are reading one of his books or attending one of his programs, the most frequent comment is: "This guy has been there, he is one of us, I am going to use these strategies."

With over 2,000 speaking engagements in all 50 states and several international locations for manufacturers, distributors and associations, you can be sure you will get the results and information you are looking for. Prior to starting his speaking career, Bob served six years in the US Navy as a Communications Specialist and then worked his way from a street sales person to the position of National Sales Manager for a Fortune 200 company.

Bob has received awards for speaking, writing and marketing too numerous to mention.

Additional Topics by Bob Oros

Why Sales People Fail

The Key to Selling Anybody

The Power of Expectations

Add Value to Every Product

How to Justify Your Price

Lost in 60 Seconds

One Good Reason to Buy

Control a Buyer's Attitude

How to Create Demand

Smoke Screen Objections

Take the Risk Out of Sales

How Small Companies Get Big